D0804974

Make:

THE MAKER MAGICIAN'S HANDBOOK

A Beginner's Guide to Magic and Making

BY MARIO MARCHESE

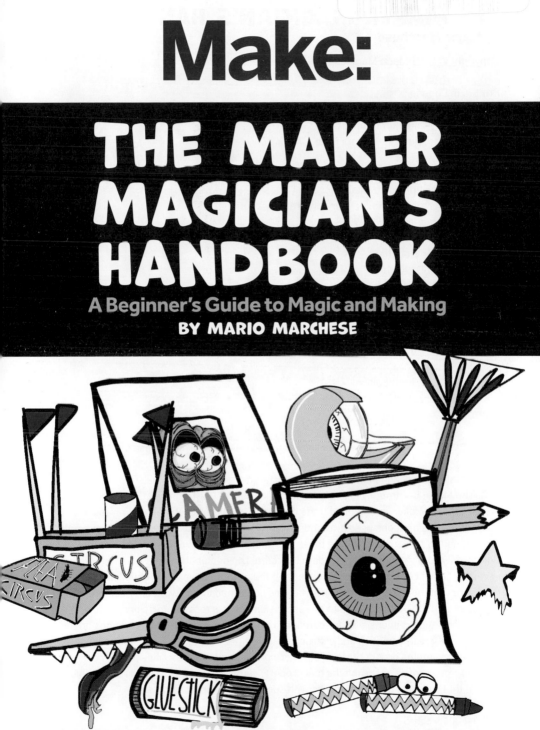

Make:
THE MAKER MAGICIAN'S HANDBOOK
By Mario Marchese

Copyright © 2021 Mario Marchese. All rights reserved.

Printed in Canada.

Published by Make Community, LLC
150 Todd Road, Suite 200, Santa Rosa, CA 95407

Make: books may be purchased for educational, business, or sales promotional use. Online editions are also available for most titles.
For more information, contact our corporate/institutional
Sales department: 800-998-9938

Publisher: Dale Dougherty
Editor: Patrick Di Justo
Copy Editor: Laurie Barton
Creative Direction/Design: Juliann Brown
Photography: Katie Rosa Marchese
Illustrations: Mario Marchese
Additional art: Adobe Stock - akrain

December 2020: First Edition
Revision History for the First Edition
11/16/2020

See www.oreilly.com/catalog/errata.csp?isbn=9781680456585 for release details.

Make:, Maker Shed, and Maker Faire are registered trademarks of Make Community, LLC. The Make: Community logo is a trademark of Make Community, LLC. *Mechanical Engineering for Makers* and related trade dress are trademarks of Make Community, LLC. Many of the designations used by manufacturers and sellers to distinguish their products are claimed as trademarks. Where those designations appear in this book, and Make Community, LLC was aware of a trademark claim, the designations have been printed in caps or initial caps. While the publisher and the authors have made good faith efforts to ensure that the information and instructions contained in this work are accurate, the publisher and the authors disclaim all responsibility for errors or omissions, including without limitation responsibility for damages resulting from the use of or reliance on this work. Use of the information and instructions contained in this work is at your own risk. If any code samples or other technology this work contains or describes are subject to open source licenses or the intellectual property rights of others, it is your responsibility to ensure that your use thereof complies with such licenses and/or rights.

978-1-68045-658-5

O'Reilly Online Learning

For more than 40 years, www.oreilly.com has provided technology and business training, knowledge, and insight to help companies succeed.

Our unique network of experts and innovators share their knowledge and expertise through books, articles, conferences, and our online learning platform. O'Reilly's online learning platform gives you on-demand access to live training courses, in-depth learning paths, interactive coding environments, and a vast collection of text and video from O'Reilly and 200+ other publishers. For more information, please visit www.oreilly.com

How to Contact Us:

Please address comments and questions concerning this book to the publisher:

Make: Community
150 Todd Road, Suite 200, Santa Rosa, CA 95407

You can also send comments and questions to us by email at books@make.co.

Make: Community is a growing, global association of makers who are shaping the future of education and democratizing innovation. Through *Make:* magazine, and 200+ annual Maker Faires, *Make:* books, and more, we share the know-how of makers and promote the practice of making in schools, libraries and homes.

To learn more about *Make:* visit us at make.co.

CONTENTS...

INTRODUCTION:
WHAT IS A MAKER MAGICIAN?

Hello! My name is Mario Marchese. My stage name is Mario the Maker Magician. I perform magic for a living! I love magic, and I love creating art that makes people believe in magic. But I didn't always know that I wanted to be a magician. In fact, I got into magic completely by accident.

MAGIC FOUND ME ...

See, I love old things. Antiques, old coffee cans, bottle caps, vintage suits, retro robots, ham radios, shortwave radios, oscilloscopes. And my favorite thing to do with old things is to make new things out of them. Treasure hunting is one of my favorite pastimes. It's like searching for new, creative possibilities around every antique shop, yard sale, or flea market corner.

It's fitting, then, that my magic journey started with an old top hat at an antique shop.

It was collapsible, like an umbrella, and the mechanics of the hat drew me to it. Inside was a label that read, "Adam." A memory sparked. As a child, I'd had a toy magic trick with Adams branding on the packaging. This was not just any old top hat ... this was a *magician's top hat*. Aside from that childhood magic trick, though, magic did not yet exist in my life. I didn't buy the hat that day, but it left an impression on my mind ... I just had this feeling that it was important. Unable to get it out of my head, I ended up returning a few days later and buying the hat. I had no idea what was about to come and the important role that hat would play in my life from there on out.

A week or so later, I visited a different antique shop (I told you, treasure hunting is my favorite pastime). I realized as I crossed the threshold that the antique shop that used to occupy the space had closed and the location was now home to a magic shop. My eyes were immediately drawn to an old TV set on the back wall. At that very moment, my favorite scene from my favorite movie was playing on that little wall-mounted TV. There was Robin Williams, playing Peter Pan in the movie *Hook*. He was sitting at a table with no food while a bunch of Lost Boys pretended to eat. Bewildered and frustrated, he picked up an empty wooden spoon and flung imaginary food across the table. BOOM — a real dollop of what looked like sherbet ice cream splatted right onto the face of Rufio, the leader of the Lost Boys. In shock, Peter was finally able to see that the whole table was filled with food. A feast of magnificent proportions.

Seeing that scene, my *favorite* movie scene of *all time*, at that moment, on that old TV in a shop I didn't even intend to enter, ended up being one of the most important moments of my entire life! It was as if the world had shifted right in front of me. I bought a few magic tricks that day and ended up returning to the shop every other day for the next year and a half of my life. An obsession was born, and the rest of my life would never be the same.

A MAKER MAGICIAN?

So that's how *magic* found me, but what does *making* mean to me?

I have always loved making things. I love taking things apart and understanding why things work and how I can replicate their movements and functions. I love carving wood, making puppets, and building small wooden boxes that can make things disappear.

I love sewing! Once, I spent three months learning how to sew my own jeans! Why would I do such a thing?! Well, I wore jeans every single day. They were a huge part of my life, and yet I absolutely took them for granted. I wanted to try to make my own pair, so I could attain some kind of grasp on this item of clothing that was so prevalent in my everyday life.

My first jeans-making attempt came out TERRIBLY! They looked like oversized clown pants that rose up way past my belly button. I tried again. This time the inseam was so low, wearing them made me waddle like a penguin. It's funny now, but at the time, two failed pairs in, it was all I could do not to give up. That's when I met a professional tailor named Manuel at my local fabric shop. He helped me. He showed me what I was doing wrong and how to correct it. He showed me how to carefully take apart an old pair of jeans and copy each piece. It took me five unwearable pairs before I finally slipped my hands into the pockets of a working pair of jeans that I'd sewn myself. And that was the first time in my life that *I understood jeans*.

That's why I love to make things. When you make something, you understand it. And when you understand something, that understanding sets you free.

I'll never forget the first time I stumbled upon *Make:* magazine, many years ago. It was an issue with a cigar box guitar on the cover. I was absolutely elated to discover that

MAKING VERSUS HACKING
To make something means to create something new from raw ingredients. To hack something means to take apart something that is made, and put it back together in a brand new way.

there was a whole magazine for and about people who love
to make things and take things apart. Flipping through those
pages gave me the same feeling as when I picked up that
magic top hat at the antique shop years before, the same
feeling as when I stumbled upon that magic shop with my
favorite scene from *Hook* playing on the old TV. I built the
cigar box guitar from the *Make:* tutorial, but more importantly,

I learned that there was a whole community of people out there like me. People to learn from, to be inspired by, and to celebrate "Aha!" maker moments with.

Make: also introduced me to the Arduino, a credit card sized piece of electronics that would open up immense possibilities for me and completely change the direction of my magic career. I had never programmed anything before, but my excitement propelled me forward with all the possibilities that come with the idea of autonomous movement in magic and theater. DIY electronics, programming, 3D printing, and handcrafting became my creative tools. Magic was my voice. I was no longer limited to what others had already created and marketed in my field. I was no longer limited to items on magic shop shelves. I was able to build whatever my mind imagined and my magic show exploded into a celebration of DIY robotics, homemade props, cardboard, recycled tin cans, and old bottle caps. I found my freedom!

I found my story.

YOUR STORY

What do *you* love to do? What gets you excited? Legos? The beach? Video games? Soccer? Skateboarding? Robots? Fashion? Within those interests are the secrets to YOUR story. And those interests might change over time. That's absolutely OK! Never shy away from learning new things at *any* point in your life. In learning, we simply expand and enrich our story!

When I was a teenager, I randomly spent three months following a sudden interest in cutting friends' hair. Why? I don't know ... I just felt it in my belly, this excitement to learn the art of DIY haircuts! Was it crazy? YES! Did I ruin people's hair? YES! Why was I interested in cutting hair? Who knows?! But during that time, I made great friendships, silly memories, and lots of laughs. It kept me busy, and it distracted me from a difficult time in my life. Creativity breeds positivity. Keep

yourself busy, keep making, keep trying new things, always. Following your excitement is so important in life.

That's not to say that you should give up at the first sign of hardship with a new project. Your goals and dreams are achievable! Keep wading, keep trudging through the obstacles. You'll realize that most goals just take hard work and the commitment to not give up. Life is not much more complicated than that! When I first dreamed of becoming a professional magician, a mentor told me that if I could master just seven routines of magic, I could make a lifetime career for myself. SEVEN. That's such a small number. You don't need to know *everything* to be great. You just need to know a few things extremely well.

I want you to find some kind of freedom through magic. I'm excited that it can be some part of your story, and I'm honored to be a part of your journey in some small way.

In the chapters to come, we'll create an entire magic show, from scratch! We'll explore the elements of a good show, we'll build our props, and we'll perform! We'll create our magic from items we can readily find in our homes, or nearby. No need for costly props ... everything I show you will be make-able and re-make-able. AND the entire show will fit inside of a SHOEBOX! You can bring it anywhere, and perform for anyone!

Practice these magic tricks in front of a mirror. Take videos and watch yourself perform them, then go back and fix the parts that don't look right.

Maybe one of the routines stands out. Think about why you like it more than the others. Maybe it reminds you of other things that make you happy. Research and figure out how your interests flow with these magic tricks. CHANGE them. ADAPT them to YOUR STORY. It's never about the tricks ... it's always about you. *Your story* will be what makes you stand out. The more you express your excitement for your interests in life, the more everyone will be excited with you!

And finally, before we begin, it's important to remember that *perfection is an illusion*. Do not be afraid to mess up! In fact, sometimes the greatest moments in show business (and life!) come from accidents ...

№ 1
LET'S START THE SHOW

All the world's a stage,
And all the men and women merely players;
They have their exits and their entrances
— *William Shakespeare*

William Shakespeare knew a thing or two about putting on a show. He knew that how you start a performance and how you end a performance are arguably the two most important parts of the show. The very first routine you do in a show has to be strong and easy for your audience to understand. If the first trick you do is too complicated, drawn out, and devoid of impact, you'll lose your audience before you even have a chance to begin.

Give yourself a chance! The opening of your show needs to be strong. It needs to grab your audience's attention, establish your character, get them on your side, and give them something to look forward to for the duration of the show.

Same goes with the ending. It's the last thing your audience will see, and the easiest part for them to remember from your show. Sometimes, even a terrible performance with an amazing ending will remain in people's memories as something great. Isn't that funny?! The goal shouldn't be to do a terrible show with a great ending, of course, but it just goes to show how *important* an ending is.

But enough show philosophy for now. Let's dive right into some MAGIC MAKING!

★ROUTINE: KNOT MAGIC!

THE EFFECT ("the effect" is just another way of saying "this is a description of the magic trick")
Make a knot magically appear on a rope. Pop the knot off the rope, and eat it! Put the rope in the bag, tear open the bag, and the rope turns into a shower of homemade confetti. Simple, strong, magical, and easily created at home! The name of the routine is a pun! Knot magic/not magic! This will come into play during the performance of the routine.

SUPPLIES
(these are the items you'll need to create your props and perform the routine)

- **2 brown paper lunch bags** I used 5⅛"×3⅛"×10⅝" bags.
- **1 large adult white cotton T-shirt** that you don't need anymore. This will be cut up to make our homemade rope! You can substitute: white clothesline rope, available at most hardware stores, or "magicians' rope," available from magic shops
- **1 piece of white tissue paper** You can substitute: plain, unlined white paper or white napkins
- **1 bag of white mini marshmallows** Beware if you have dietary restrictions, as you will eat this during the routine. You can skip this part, if necessary!
- **Optional: markers, crayons, paper, glue, glitter** and/or anything you'd like to use to add some decoration!

BUILD (instructions to create your props)
MAKE THE MAGIC ROPE
Rope is a classic prop in magic. You can buy "magician's rope" from magic shops, but for this project, I want to show you how

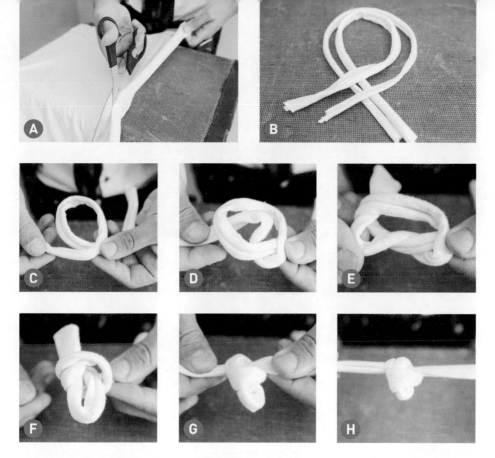

to improvise by using objects found in our homes. Let's start with our white cotton T-shirt. We're going to cut a few long strips from the shirt to create our homemade rope.

1. Cut a few strips ... 18"–25" long and 2"–4" wide (Figures Ⓐ and Ⓑ).

As you'll see, the T-shirt cotton will naturally roll into a rope-type shape and it is super soft and flexible, perfect for our Knot Magic purposes.

2. Tie a slipknot

A slipknot is a fake knot! It looks like a real knot, but when you pull the rope from both ends, the knot vanishes. We need to tie a slipknot on one end of our homemade rope like you see in Figures Ⓒ through Ⓗ.

Practice tying the slipknot and pulling the rope free several times, so you can do it easily and without hesitation.

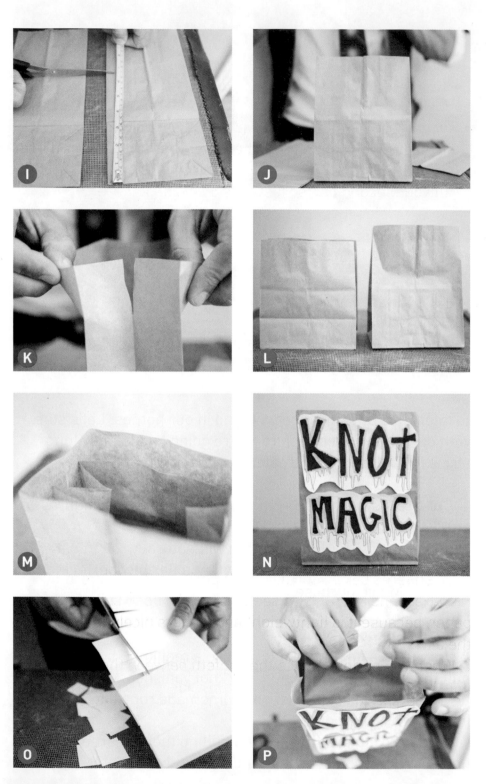

3. Prep your bag

We need to make our bag as efficient as possible for the trick. To do so, trim one bag down, so it stands 6½" high (Figures **I** and **J**).

- Cut a 2" slit from the top down on both sides of the bag. This will secure the bag to tear where we want so the confetti can come out (Figure **K**)!
- Cut your second bag so it stands 5¾" high (Figure **L**).
- Place the shorter bag inside the taller one and set the bags aside for now (Figure **M**).
- Now, decorate the outside of your bag, if you'd like (Figure **N**). There are no rules here! Make it your own. Express your own style and personality. Think about how you'd like your show to look. Your style will probably evolve as you develop your character and perform more and more. Maybe you prefer to keep it plain and simple. Maybe you'd like to label it with its name, like I did. The great thing about this trick is that you re-make it each time you perform it, so you're never locked into one style.

4. Create the confetti

Take your white tissue paper (or substitute material) and cut it into 1" squares (Figure **O**). They don't need to be perfect. Make a bunch! The more you use, the bigger the confetti explosion when you perform! I usually use about 25 to 50 squares per performance. Experiment with different materials and amounts to see what works best. I like tissue paper, because it is lightweight and flutters nicely through the air.

When you're done, place the confetti *between* the two bags (Figure **P**), positioning it on the front side, the side that will face the audience when you perform.

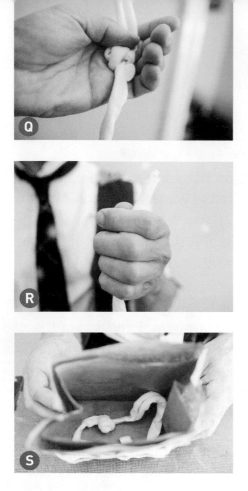

5. Learn a finger palm

For this routine, you'll need to know how to hide your knot and marshmallow in a position called a *finger palm*. To do that, hold the items as shown in Figures **Q** and **R**.

As you see, the slipknot and marshmallow (the marshmallow will be your mock knot!) are now hidden on the inside of your middle, ring, and pinky fingers. The marshmallow should be under the knot. The top of the rope comes out of your hand between your index and thumb. Make sure your hand is positioned so that the sneaky part is hidden from your audience.

What is the best way to get this right? Practice, practice, practice in front of a mirror! I spend a LOT of time practicing in front of mirrors before ever performing a new routine in front of a live audience. For me, the next step after mirror-work is video! I take lots of videos of my magic, so I can see different angles, etc. After that, I perform for close family or friends (usually my wife and kids!). Only after I'm confident in front of them, will I finally debut a new trick in front of an audience. Take the time to practice your moves. It will be well worth it!

6. Prep the props for performance time

Prepare a rope with a slipknot, and place it inside the innermost bag along with one mini marshmallow (Figure **S**). Confetti should already be in place in between the bag layers.

Place the bag gently on its side inside of your shoebox until you're ready to perform.

THE PERFORMANCE (step by step instructions on how to perform the actual routine)

1. Remove your prepared bag from the shoebox, close the shoebox lid, and place the bag on top of the box, with the side of the bag loaded with confetti toward your audience.

2. "What you are about to witness is ... Knot Magic!" you announce. (You'll notice that this is a play on words. Did the audience think you said "knot magic" or did they think you said "not magic"?

This actually should be part of the trick. They should not be able to tell the difference!)

3. Reach into the bag and remove the rope, hiding the marshmallow and knot in a finger palm, as we learned before. Remember, the marshmallow should be *under* the knot. With this simple move, you are creating magic before you even start the routine! The audience thinks you are only holding a rope, but you are already two steps ahead of them (Figure **U**)!

4. Grab the loose end of the rope with your other hand (Figure **V** on the following page), and grasp it with the hand that is holding the knot and marshmallow, so that the rope is now in

a loop (Figure **W**).

5. Dip the rope partially into the bag and release the unknotted end into the bag (Figure **X**).

6. Swirl the rope end in the bag as if you are trying to knot it. Slowly pull the rope out ... no knot (Figure **Y**)!

7. Say: "This is ... not magic," while shaking your head in disappointment.

8. Do the same exact thing again. This time swirling even more, desperately trying to make a knot appear.

9. Pull the rope out ... still no knot! Again: "This is not magic ..."

10. The third time, bring your hand down into the bag once again, *but this time* let go of the knotted end, while using the same swirling movements as before. Be careful not to let go of the marshmallow, though!

You've conditioned your audience to believe there will, once again, be no knot, but this time, after swirling the rope around, slowly pull it out of the bag to reveal THE KNOT, which has now magically appeared at the end of the rope (Figures **Z** and **Aa**)!

"Knot magic!"

Practice, practice, practice. The switch must be done smoothly, with no visible change in your movements. Hide the sneaky move within the bag! You should have your pinky and ring finger inside the bag as you move down to up, releasing the knot end.

You *could* end the trick right here! But we're going to take it a step further.

It's time to make the knot *disappear*, and we're going to do that by ... EATING IT! You'll probably have figured out by now that we'll actually be eating the marshmallow, not the cloth rope. But, how do we make the switch?

You'll remember that when we first took the rope out of the bag, we hid a mini marshmallow under the knot in our finger palm. When we let go of the knot, we kept the marshmallow hidden in our finger palm.

At this point, the knot should still be dangling at the end of our rope.

1. With your empty hand, pick up the end of the rope with the knot, and position it in your other hand, with the knot resting against the hidden marshmallow (Figures **Bb**, **Cc**, and **Dd**).

2. Pause. Then, smoothly and imperceptibly pull the other end of the rope, undoing the slipknot (Figures **Ee**, **Ff**, and **Gg**). This is another move that takes practice! You don't want your audience to see that you've undone the knot!

3. Now, pinch the rope and marshmallow between your index finger and thumb. It will look like you're holding the knot. Your audience will not suspect that you actually have a marshmallow pinched between your fingers! Pinching them together creates the *illusion* that the knot is still there.

4. I like to slowly shake the rope a little as I show both marshmallow and rope. Pause. Now grab the rope with the other hand, holding it in a loop shape (Figure **Hh**).

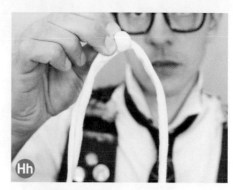

5. Pull the marshmallow off with the other hand. Tug it right off with a natural tug, as if it popped right off the rope (Figure **Ii**)! Flash it quickly to the audience, and then *eat it* (Figure **Jj**)! This is a great and unexpected moment! You made a knot appear like magic. You magically popped the knot right off the rope, and then you ATE IT! What?!

Kk

Ll

6. As you chew the marshmallow, slowly gather your rope, and put it inside the innermost bag.

7. Pick up the bag with one hand, and as you do so, pinch the inner bag *closed* with your fingers. Hold the bag from the top back, with your thumb on the outside and fingers in (Figure **Kk**). The audience does not know that it's a double bag and will not suspect that you are hiding an additional layer, if you hold it properly. (Again, practice.)

8. With your free hand, grip the front of the outside bag (Figure **Ll**).

9. Blow in the bag as you tear it open! The confetti will fly out creating an awesome ending! As the confetti flutters, crumble the bag into a ball, and take your bow! Well done!

ADDING MUSIC

One of the greatest ways to enhance a magical performance is with music. What are your favorite songs and types of music? Think about the kind of music you personally love to hear, and play around with it. Try performing this routine along to your favorite song. Different types of music will set completely different moods in your show. What type of mood do you want your audience to experience? Personally, I love pop punk and old-time circus music, and I mix those all throughout my theater show. I've even synced some of my robotics to certain musical tracks.

Allow yourself to play with the pace and rhythm of the music as you perform. Try to make the knot appear at a specific part of the song. Don't just perform with music in the background ... let the music be a part of the routine.

Playing the song over and over again as you practice can even help you memorize the routine more easily, as your brain will begin to associate the moves with moments in the song. It can help you gain more confidence ... give it a try!

№2
FINDING OUR GROOVE

We've successfully opened our show, and introduced our audience to our character and to the tone of the show. Now they're ready to see more! We're now in the zone of the show where it's important to find our groove and settle into a mood. We can play with pacing and variety that will keep the audience interested right up to the midway point in our show.

★ROUTINE: FLEA CIRCUS COIN MAGIC

Flea circuses are fascinating. Imagine a real circus with a tightrope act, a trapeze, and more, but all in miniature and supposedly run by tiny insects! The flea circus has its roots as a classic vaudeville and sideshow act. Magicians have long taken elements of the flea circus and adapted them into their own acts, too.

Now, I present to you the Flea Circus Toilet Roll Coin Vanish! That's right. You heard it here first, folks. A Toilet Paper Roll Coin Vanish performed by fleas! Don't worry ... no fleas were harmed during the production of this trick. (There are no real fleas involved at all in a modern-day flea circus, as a matter of fact!)

This is the second routine of our show, and we're changing the pace a little, to keep our audience on their toes. In fact, we will be inviting our audience to join us right at our table!

THE EFFECT A coin disappears right before our audience's eyes and re-appears in a spectator's hand, flea circus style.

SUPPLIES

- **1 brown paper lunch bag** I use a 5⅛"×3⅛"×10⅝" bag, the same size bag used in Knot Magic.
- **1 toilet paper tube**
- **1 glue stick**
- **Any type of tape, clear or masking**

- **1 sheet of 8½"×11" unlined thick white card stock paper** You can substitute: 1 sheet of 8½"×11" unlined white printer paper
- **1 EMPTY matchbox** We'll need the type of matchbox with a sliding drawer. (It is worth the effort to find a matchbox like this ... it can create great magic!)
- **2 quarters that look alike** You can substitute: any two matching coins that are smaller than the diameter of the toilet paper tube
- **Crayons and markers**
- **Optional: 4 straws**

BUILD
PREP THE PAPER BAG

1. First, we'll need to shorten our brown paper bag down to around 3" tall. We want the bag to be shorter than the toilet paper tube (Figure **A**).

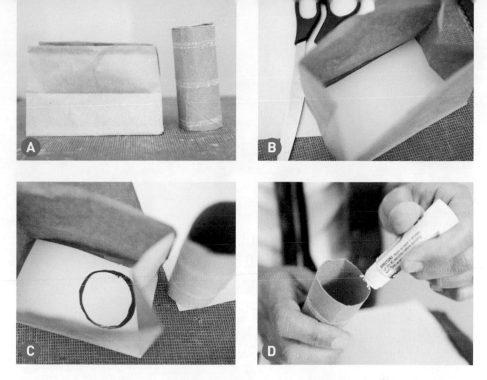

2. Now, cut a rectangular piece of white card stock paper that will fit snugly inside the bottom of the paper bag (Figure **B**).

3. With a dark colored marker, make a circle slightly larger than the diameter of the toilet paper tube, on one side of the rectangular card stock insert.

4. Insert the card stock, circle side up, snugly inside the bottom of the paper bag (Figure **C**).

HACK THE TOILET PAPER TUBE

In this routine, the toilet paper tube will be our gimmick. (Makers hack things, magicians gimmick things. It's the same idea.) A gimmicked item is one that carries a hidden secret which helps in the magic of a trick. We're going to hack, or gimmick, our toilet paper tube!

1. Apply glue all along one circular opening edge of the tube (Figure **D**). We want this glue to be invisible when dry, so we'll use something like school glue stick rather than, say, hot glue.

2. Press the glued end of the tube to the unused portion of our white card stock (Figure **E**). After the glue is completely dry and the tube is securely attached to the paper, carefully cut the paper around the outside of the tube, as close to the edge as possible (Figure **F**).

Our tube now has a paper bottom (Figure **G**).

> **NOTE:** If you are using regular printer paper rather than the thicker card stock paper, repeat the gluing and cutting out process one more time, to double up the paper on the bottom of the tube and make it more opaque.

3. Now, our toilet paper tube is successfully gimmicked! We'll want to keep the paper bottom a secret from our audience, so be careful how you position and handle the tube.

4. Place your gimmicked tube upright in the paper bag, *gimmicked side down*, next to the circle we drew earlier (Figure **H**). The paper bottom of the tube should be imperceptible now.

PREP THE MATCHBOX

1. Slide the drawer out of the empty matchbox. Now, this next step is a little tricky to explain, so you may need to rely on the

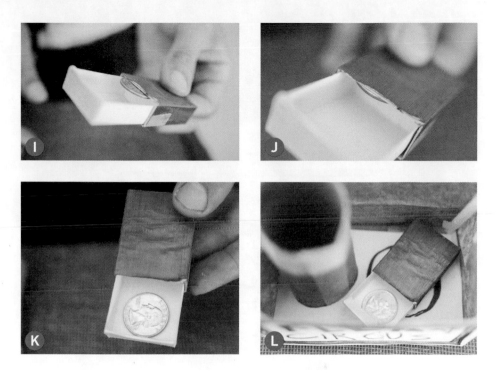

photos. We're going to hide one of our quarters inside the box, by wedging it in between the lip of the back edge of the drawer and the top of the box (Figure **I**). Slide the drawer partially in, so the quarter stays firmly stuck in place, yet the box *appears* to be open and empty (Figure **J**). This alone is already a powerful illusion!

When you close the drawer, the quarter will fall in, so the next time you open the matchbox, there will be a quarter in the drawer. Go ahead, give it a try!

2. Now set it back up again, quarter wedged and hidden, drawer partially open. Take your *second* quarter and place it inside the matchbox drawer, visible (Figure **K**).

3. Leave the matchbox just like that, drawer partially open, with one quarter wedged and hidden and one quarter visible in the drawer. Place it in the bag on top of your drawn circle, next to the toilet paper tube (Figure **L**).

DECORATE THE FLEA CIRCUS

Now that we've built the working parts of the trick, it's time to design the look of our flea circus (Figure M)! The way something looks really can impact an audience, and flea circuses in particular are known for the interesting and mysterious ways they look. The more elaborate, the more intrigue and curiosity you create. They're often meant to mimic the look of a classic circus, just in miniature. Have fun with your design. Use markers, crayons, paint ... whatever you'd like. Use the paper remnants attached to straws to create little flags! Don't forget to decorate your matchbox and toilet paper tube, too!

THE PERFORMANCE

It's time to perform the flea circus routine! Invite your audience to join you around your table. For this routine, you can even be completely surrounded without risking the revelation of any secrets!

1. Explain to your audience that you'd like to introduce them to something from another era, a nod to a time when tiny *insects* performed whole circus shows!

Feel free to get right into a circus ringleader persona here:

"Step right up! Step right up! Come see the Circus in Miniature!"

2. Explain that you have a world famous flea. (Give your famous flea a name! Make it come to life for your audience! For the sake of this explanation, we'll call him ... Francesco.)

"Francesco is a world famous magic flea who can vanish anything that fits inside of this tube!"

3. Carefully take out the matchbox and hold it tilted downward so everyone sees the visible quarter (Figure **N**).

4. Ask a spectator to hold out their hand, "You! Please! Hold your hand out!" Visibly dump the quarter from the matchbox drawer into their hand, and ask them to place the quarter inside the drawn circle in the flea circus. (Do not yet close the drawer of the matchbox! Also, it's a good idea for you to keep the toilet paper tube steady with your hand (Figure **O**), so the spectator doesn't accidentally knock it over and reveal the gimmicked bottom as they place the quarter next to it.)

5. Tell everyone to look in the flea circus and make sure they see the coin!

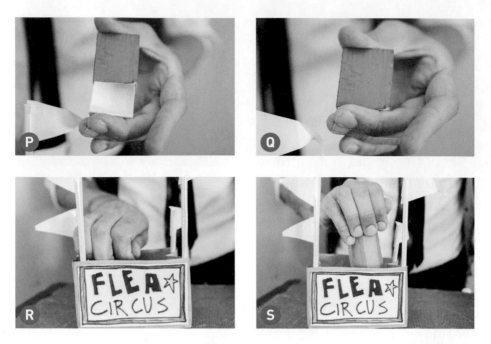

6. Now, you have a seemingly empty matchbox in your hand. Call on another spectator, "You! Can you please hold your hand out?"

7. Show the matchbox empty to everyone (Figure **P**), then push the drawer closed (Figure **Q**). (Remember, the wedged coin will fall into the drawer when you close it!)

8. Place the matchbox in your spectator's open hand, and ask them to cover the matchbox with their other hand.

9. Here comes the fun. Make sure everyone sees the coin still in the drawn circle in the paper bag flea circus.

10. Then tell everyone that you have Francesco the Flea right in your pocket! Pretend to gently take Francesco out of your pocket and carefully drop the flea inside the toilet paper tube.
Have everyone look inside the tube.
"Can you see it? Can you see it? The Great Francesco! Can

you see it!?"

11. Now, cover the top of the toilet paper tube with the palm of your hand. Explain that you don't want Francesco to jump out!

12. Gripping the tube with your palm (Figure **R**), gently and slightly lift the tube and place it over the quarter in the drawn circle. (Figure **S**) Remember, the audience has no idea that the tube has a paper bottom!

13. With your free hand, wave your fingers at the flea circus! Say, "Francesco is tickling me! I think it's working!"

14. Slowly lift your hand off the top of the tube and say, "Look! Look! Is the coin there?"
     They look and see nothing (Figure **T**)! We know that this is because the coin is hidden underneath our gimmick, but to your audience, it has simply disappeared! Don't rush this moment! Have the audience look in the tube to confirm the

coin is really gone.

"Francesco did it! Wow! It's gone!"

15. Tell everyone to grab some magic and shake their hands. Tell the person holding the matchbox to do it, too. Then say, "Wait! Wait ... did you hear that?!"

16. Point to the person holding the matchbox, "Listen! Listen!"

17. They shake the matchbox again, and the coin can be heard. Have them open the box. You never touch the box ... let the magic happen all in their hands. The coin is there (Figures **U**)!

"Oh no!" you say. Francesco was in there with the coin, too!" Pretend to grab the flea from the spectator's shoulder and shout, "Applause for my helper and for Francesco!"

As they applaud, you applaud, accidentally "squishing" Francesco.

"Oh no! Francesco! What have I done?!" This is an old flea circus bit that can make for a great, funny ending to a flea circus routine.

PACK UP:

Place the box back in the bag. You can give the coin away to the person who helped you, or place the coin in the matchbox and close it. This will help when you put everything back in the bag so the two coins don't clink together and reveal the secret as you put the routine away. These little details are important to pay attention to. A routine can be fantastic, but if we are careless when putting items away and accidentally reveal a secret, the magic is gone. Be mindful of your props, even

when you're not actively performing the routine!

Our next routine includes an element of *failure*, but don't worry ... it's intentional! The idea of failure is not uncommon in magic. Magicians pretend to fail so that when the magic finally does happen, the surprise is even greater. We explored this in the Knot Magic routine as well! This element of failure is a fun concept to keep in mind when creating your own routines.

Another concept in creating a great show is the exploration of many different elements throughout. Instead of doing a whole show with one type of prop, changing it up helps keep the audience engaged. At this point in our homemade magic show, we've already done magic with rope, we've done magic with coins, and now we're going to perform with cards!

★ROUTINE: THE CARD MACHINE

> **NOTE:** "This is an adaptation of "Rising Card From Envelope" by Bill Severn and Pete Biro; *Tarbell Course in Magic Vol.7*, page 121"

THE EFFECT

The magician has a spectator select a random playing card. Then they have the spectator place the card back in the deck, *and* have the spectator mix up the deck. The magician places the cards into a contraption called a Card Machine. A card mysteriously rises, but it's the wrong card. Within a flash the wrong card instantly changes into ... the selected card!

SUPPLIES

- **2 packs of the same playing cards**
- **1 envelope** I used a 3⅝"×6½" envelope.
- **1 pencil**
- **A bunch of rubber bands**
- **Markers or crayons**
- **Scissors**

BUILD

PREP THE ENVELOPE

1. Seal your empty envelope.

2. Line up a playing card along the side of the envelope, for sizing, and cut the envelope about ½" past the card (Figure **A**).

3. Turn the envelope so the open end faces up. About ¾" below the open end, cut or tear small half circles on either side (Figure **B**). This is so a pencil can slide through, but size-wise the hole should be wide enough to fit two pencils.

4. Outline both sides of your envelope with a dark color (Figure **C**).

Now, make it your own! Create the look of your Card Machine! I chose to draw gears on one side, with images of a 9V battery, wires, buttons, and switches (Figure **D**). You can do something similar or make the design completely your own. On the other side of the envelope as shown in Figure **E** I wrote "Card Machine!" Get creative! Think about how you want your Card Machine to look, and think also of the overall look of your show. Your props should all look like they belong with each other. They don't need to "match" exactly, but they should complement each other: battery and wires, or stars and planets, or birds and flowers, or whatever. This helps create a cohesive theme to your show.

HACK THE PENCIL

1. It's gimmick time! Take a few rubber bands and twist and wrap them onto the middle of your pencil. You'll need to add enough rubber bands to create about ¼" of rubber banding all around (Figure **F**). I have three or four wide rubber bands on my pencil.

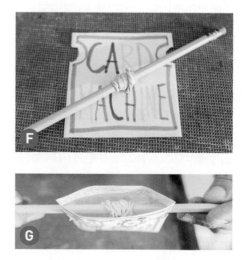

2. Slide your pencil carefully through the two holes you created in the envelope, so that the rubber banded area is now hidden inside the envelope (Figure **G**).

THE PERFORMANCE

Now, how do we know which card is selected? How do we perform the trick? The secret is that we need to do something called *forcing a card*. That means that we will actually *make* the spectator choose the card we want them to choose.

We need two of the same exact card. That's why this trick requires us to have two matching decks of cards! Make sure the pattern on the backs of the cards is exactly the same. The first step is to choose which card you want the audience to pick for the trick.

I chose the jack of hearts, for example.

1. Take one jack of hearts from one pack and slide it into the Card Machine, so that the back of the card is against the back wall of the inside of the envelope, and the face of the jack is against the rubber bands (Figure **H**).

2. We don't want the audience to ever see this extra card. When the Card Machine is resting on your table, always make sure the opening of the envelope is facing you. When you pick up the Card Machine for your performance, you'll want to pinch both the jack of hearts and the envelope together (Figure **I**).

3. The second jack of hearts goes on top of the deck of cards that you will be using in the routine (Figure **J**). That will be your *force card*.

So, you have the jack of hearts on top of the deck. You have your Card Machine resting on your performance table with the opening facing you. And the second jack of hearts is hiding in the envelope. You're ready to go!

4. Hold the cards face down in a *dealers grip*, as shown in Figure **K**.

Remember, the jack of hearts should be on top, facing down.

5. Have a spectator pick up a small portion of cards from the top of the deck, flip them over, so they are now face up, and put them back on top of the deck, still face up (Figure **L**).

6. Say, "This is a random card!" pointing to the one on top. And say, "Now, pick up a bigger pile of cards, flip them over, and put them on top again." (Figure **M**)

"This is another random card!"

7. Slowly spread the deck face up, showing the audience that the cards are all mixed up, some face up, some face down (Figure **N**).

8. When you reach the first face down card, stop, and have your spectator memorize that card and show the rest of the audience, while you avert your eyes (Figure **O**).

That will be the jack of hearts, and your audience will not suspect that the selected card was not random. You've officially forced a card! Try it out yourself!

NOTE: This method of forcing a card comes from "The Cut Deeper Force" by Ed Balducci and Ken Krenzal; *Hugards Magic Monthly Vol. 14, No. 6*, pg. 502; November 1956.

9. After the audience has seen the card and the spectator has memorized it, give someone else the pack of cards, ask them to fix the cards and shuffle the selected card in, making sure it is not on the top or the bottom of the deck, but mixed somewhere within. When everything is shuffled, take the cards back, and explain that you have no idea what card they picked nor where it is in the deck!

10. Now, pick up the Card Machine, pinching the second jack of hearts and envelope.

11. Take a pack of around 15 cards from the top of the deck, and insert them in the Card Machine, on the opposite side of the pencil from where the jack of hearts is hiding. Make sure the cards are facing the same way as the jack of hearts (Figure **P**).

12. Turn the envelope around, without showing the inside, and hold the Card Machine by the pencil on each side (Figure **Q**).

13. Ask your spectator to name their card aloud! After they do so, count, "One, two, three," as you move your arms down to up with each number. On the third movement, twist the pencil *toward yourself* (Figure **R**). The wrong card will rise! (Remember ... element of failure!)

14. Ask, "Is this your card?" Obviously, they will say no.

15. Keep that card in the Card Machine, risen about three-quarters up. Move your arms up and down again, as you count to three again. This time, swiftly twist the pencil *away from you*, and two things will happen simultaneously ... the wrong card will spin down into the envelope, and the correct card will rise up! The jack of hearts (Figure **S**)!

As always, practice this move in front of a mirror! When you coordinate your movements well and twist the pencil with the right amount of speed, it really does look like magic! Experiment with how many cards to put in your Card Machine and how many rubber bands to wrap around your pencil to find the perfect combination to create the level of pressure and grip needed to successfully perform this move.

ALTERNATE VERSION

Essentially, we've created a gear with the rubber bands around the pencil. Hack it, tinker with it, think of new ideas! Create a routine of your own! Maybe you want the right card to rise right away! If that's the case, place a chunk of cards right behind the jack of hearts. Experiment with this: Instead of twisting the pencil with your fingers, hold onto the pencil with one hand, and flick the envelope with your other fingers, so it spins around around the pencil. If you spin the envelope with the right force, and in the right direction, by the time the envelope makes its full revolution, the jack of hearts will be sticking out (Figures **T**, **U**, **V**, and **W**)! Centrifugal force keeps the cards in place upside down. The spinning causes the "gear" to push the selected card out.

№3
WOW THEM

My goal with this book is not just to give you a bunch of magic tricks. My goal is to help you understand the *song* of a *show*. What makes a show a show instead of just a series of tricks? It's about understanding the chorus, the verse, the bridge, and the breakdown. A great show blends each routine together seamlessly. Every transition makes sense, every problem is solved, and it all comes together in cohesion. And this is what our next routine is about ... bringing it all together. We're in the middle of our show, we're reaching a crescendo.

★ROUTINE:
THE BALANCING TOWER OF AWESOMENESS

Our show began with a piece of rope that transformed into confetti. We went on to create an illusion in miniature. We got everyone out of their seats. We shifted our format and pace to keep our audience engaged. Once we firmly earned their attention, we found a selected card from a shuffled deck with a homemade Card Machine. Now, let's take an element from each of those routines and blend it into one great feat of magic.

THE EFFECT

Various elements from our show thus far will be carefully constructed into an impossibly balanced Tower of Awesomeness, including the very playing card that was chosen from our previous routine.

SUPPLIES

- **1 brown paper lunch bag** this should match the dimensions of the paper bag in our Knot Magic routine, but no need to gimmick this one. I used a 5⅛"×3⅛"×10⅝" bag, trimmed down to about 6½" high.
- **1 toilet paper tube** this should match the toilet paper tube from our Flea Circus routine, but no need to gimmick it. If you decorated that tube, decorate this one to match!
- **1 playing card box** this should match the box from the deck of cards used in the Card Machine routine.
- **1 quarter**
- **2 playing cards** the forced card from the Card Machine routine plus another random card
- **Scotch tape**
- **Scissors**
- **1 Funny Flower** the Funny Flower is actually a prop from the next chapter in this book. Skip ahead, build it, then come back here!

BUILD
PREP YOUR PROPS

1. Start by placing the quarter inside the empty playing card box (Figure **A** on the following page). Close the top.

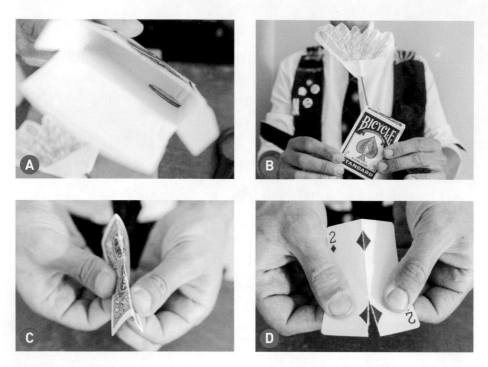

2. Slide the Funny Flower inside the box (Figure **B**).

3. Put the card box with the quarter and flower inside of the paper bag, along with the toilet paper tube.

HACK THE CARD

For this routine, we need to gimmick our forced playing card, so that it can stand up on its own. Let's build it!

1. Take the *random* playing card and carefully fold it lengthwise, like a hot dog bun (Figure **C**). Match the ends perfectly and press. Open and close it a few times, back and forth, and the card will begin to split. Carefully tear it in half (Figure **D**).

2. Line up one of the halves to the back of the forced playing card (Figure **E**). In this book we used the jack of hearts. Use a flat surface to line it all up and carefully tape it down in the

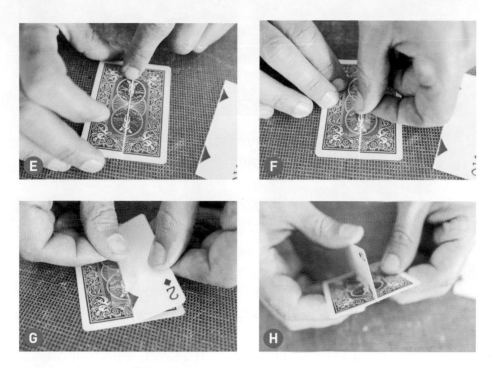

middle (Figure **F**). The tape acts like a hinge. Turn the flap to the other side, and secure it with another piece of tape, so both sides of our "hinged flap" are reinforced (Figures **G** and **H**).

THE PERFORMANCE

1. Right after you perform the Card Machine routine, place your props back into your shoebox, making sure to retain the gimmicked jack of hearts for the next trick. Change your music to something dramatic and upbeat. Remove your paper bag from the box and open it up, standing it up. Set it aside.

2. Take out the toilet paper tube, bring it up to your eye, and look through it like a telescope. With this subtlety — don't spell it out in words — you are showing that the tube is, in fact, see-through, further solidifying the mystery from your Flea Circus routine. The audience doesn't know that this is a second tube. Set the tube aside.

3. Next, pull out the closed playing card box with the quarter and the Funny Flower. Set it aside.

4. Remove the (gimmicked) forced card and show it to the audience. Remind them that this was the card that they had selected! Show the face of the card to the audience as you keep the flap pressed against the back of the card, hidden.

5. Reposition the open paper bag front and center.

6. Now, show both sides of the card, in a swift, fluid motion, so as not to reveal the flap. We want our audience to be confident that these objects are normal and unaltered. As long as your hand stays in motion as you turn the card, the gimmick will be undetectable.

7. Now, bring the card behind the bag, and deftly open the flap, so the card creates a "T" shape and can stand on its own behind the bag (Figure **I**).

8. Next pick up the toilet paper tube. Again, show the audience the inside of the tube. Carefully position the tube on top of the card, balancing securely (Figure **J**).

9. Next pick up your playing card box with the quarter and Funny Flower inside. Show both sides of the box. Behind the lunch bag, carefully nestle a bottom corner of the box inside the top of the toilet paper tube. The box will rest balanced on an angle (Figure **K**). The hidden quarter inside helps it stay balanced, by adding some weight. The flower stem should be poking out of the top corner for best balance. This will take a little practice! Practice, practice, practice! It is worth the effort to be able to perform this seamlessly!

10. You'll notice that at this point, the flower will be sticking up higher than the paper bag (Figure **L**). Slowly remove the bag to reveal ... the Balancing Tower Of Awesomeness (Figure **M**)! This is a strong moment and should not be rushed. The longer your audience soaks this in, the more amazing it becomes. Let it breathe. Let them have that moment.

11. When you're ready, pinch the playing card closed as you pick it up in one hand, while picking up the toilet paper tube with the other

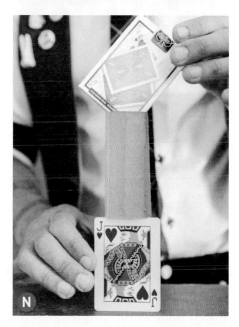

hand. Pull both objects to the sides and let the tower collapse (Figure **N**). Place each object back into the bag. Show the playing card, front and back, again, before putting it away, again pinching the flap closed to hide it. Again, show the tube empty before putting it away. Toss the box in the bag, but hold onto the Funny Flower. That comes next ...

№ 4
CHANGE IT UP/ GET SILLY

We've done some great magic already, and created more than just a collection of tricks ... we've tied each routine to the others. We're making our own props! We're learning how to involve our audience and make it an interactive experience for them. In other words, we're building a show! As a performer, my goal is always to bring some type of new surprise with each routine that I perform.

This next section of the show is all about being silly. Yes, there is actually an art to being silly, and there are people in the world who actually do it for a living! Imagine that ... having a job to make people laugh! There are comedians, talk show hosts, comedy magicians, and even comedy maker magicians! Making people laugh is something I love so much. Let's show the audience what being a professionally silly person means!

★ROUTINE: FUNNY FLOWER

THE EFFECT
Make a paper flower magically wilt (or headbang!!) at your command!

This is one of my go-to homemade magic treasures. You can amaze people and make people laugh at the same time, all using materials you can readily find in your home. I'm giving you three versions here, but the variations and possibilities are endless!

SUPPLIES

- **1 plastic ziplock bag** A 6½" wide sandwich bag with green tabs works best.
- **1 sheet of blank paper**
- **Crayons, markers, or colored pencils**
- **Clear Scotch tape**
- **Scissors**
- **Optional: crepe paper roll for tissue flower variation**

BUILD
MAKE THE STEM

1. We need to separate the zip portion of the sandwich bag from the rest of the bag to make a "stem" for our flower. To do so, cut along the edge of the ziplock portion, starting from the clear bag side (Figure Ⓐ).

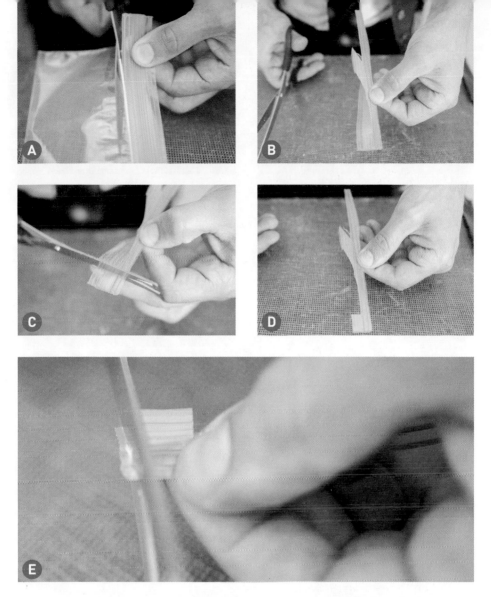

2. Now, cut along the other side of the zip, to remove the green portion, but be sure to leave a small tab of green at the bottom, which will serve as a grip for your thumb during performance. Also cut out a leaf shape in the green tab about halfway up the strip. Once cut, spread the leaf apart (Figures **B**, **C**, and **D**)!

3. To finish off our "stem," cut a bit off the end of the thumb tab at the bottom (Figure **E**). This is very important, because it will allow us to do the magic move during performance!

ADD THE PETALS

1. Next, it's time to create the top, the petals, of our flower! One way to do this is to simply cut out a proportionately sized triangle of blank paper (Figure **F**) and color it in like a flower (Figure **G**)!

2. Then, tape your flower head to the top of your stem, the side without the thumb tab. Tuck the tape around the bottom of the paper flower head, and your prop is complete (Figures **H** and **I**)!

LEARN THE SECRET MOVE

1. Hold the flower by the tab at the bottom of the stem, between your thumb and first three fingers. Make sure your

fingers are facing your audience, and your thumb is hidden ... this will protect your secret move (Figure **J**). Now, squeeze the tab tight and slowly push your thumb up. The flower will mysteriously begin to bow down (Figure **K**)! This is because the bag is sealed by a track, and since we snipped the bottom of the track, it is now free to slide.

THE PERFORMANCE

1. Try something like: "People of all ages! HERE HERE! I am the great MAKER MAGICIAN from the faraway land of [your town] — here to perform for you one of the GREATEST mysteries of our time. This is a flower! That I made! This flower has power! FLOWER POWER! Watch how I can control this flower with my mind! When I say DOWN, the flower will go down! When I say UP, it will rise!"

2. Slowly make a low pitched sound like, "ohhhhhhhhhhhhhhhmmmmmmmmmmmmmm," and as you make that sound, slowly push your thumb up to make the flower sink down (Figure **L**). When it reaches its lowest point, pause (Figure **M**). Then change your sound to a really high pitched annoying tone, "ahhhhhhhhhhhhhhhhhhhhh!" and slide your thumb back down to slowly make the flower rise again (Figure **N**)!

You can move from that right into a second phase of performance. This bit is an old vaudeville clown gag that fits perfectly with our headbanging flower:

3. Stare at the flower and say, "I will now attempt to blow the flower down!" Take a deep dramatic breath in and blow at the flower. Nothing happens. Take another dramatic breath in and blow at the flower again. Nothing happens. On the third try, take another deep breath in and as *you breathe in* make the flower go down! Look at the flower and say, "HUH???!"

Another funny gag: Look at your audience and say, "I can control this flower with my mind!" Look at your flower and command it to go down. Nothing happens. Say a little more firmly, "Flower, go down!" Nothing happens. Shout, "FLOWER GO DOWN!" Nothing happens. Now, look to your audience and say, "Why isn't it going down?" As you say that, make the flower go down while you're not looking. The audience will see the flower going down and shout at you. Repeat this until the audience starts getting restless. Three times is usually a charm.

ALTERNATE VERSIONS
The Tissue Rose: You can create a beautiful 3D version of the flower we created earlier, using crepe paper twirled into a realistic rose. I like to create a vase full of these, then spontaneously pluck one from the vase to perform with. Keep

your vase full for whenever company is over! Touches like this can make your magic even more memorable.

1. Start by pinching your crepe paper between your index finger and thumb. From the bottom twist and turn, twist and turn. You are rolling the tissue tight, creating a stem shape, keeping the top part of the crepe paper open to form the petals of your flower. With your other hand, feed the paper slowly, allowing the flower to take shape (Figures **O** and **P**).

2. Once the flower feels like the right size, carefully fluff open the flower as you pinch the bottom together. Tape it to the top of your stem using Scotch tape (Figure **Q**). Perform just as explained before!

Headbanging Robot: This is really cool! The truth is that our routine doesn't need to be a flower at all! I want you to know that once you learn something new, whether it's a magic trick, a programming project, a new recipe, or what have you ... you can HACK them, and make them your OWN! Take something apart! Re-create! Innovate! When someone teaches you how

to do something, that should be the *start* of your creativity ... Keep going! I heard someone say once that we should always strive to make the best better. This can be adapted to anything creative! What will you create??

I happen to love robots, so for this version of the routine, I made a headbanging robot out of paper and taped it to a "stem" without the leaf detail. You can even make two robots and have one in each hand, both headbanging to music! Take a video and make it into a headbanging robot GIF!

Magicians go to great lengths to create a single magic trick. You might see an amazing magic routine — maybe something disappearing or floating in the air — that only lasts a few seconds. The truth is, a lot of preparation and *practice* happens long before those few seconds of magic are ever even presented. Take your time and perfect your work. Each and every moment of your presentation is important. And remember ... there's more than just amazement in magic. Making someone laugh is just as memorable as doing something amazing. And making someone feel special is just as significant, too. The reason magic is so important in the world is because it shakes us out of the ordinary. It makes us question reality. Even if it only lasts for a few seconds, those few seconds are pure beauty. This simple flower routine has the potential to tap into all three: doing something amazing, making people laugh, and making people feel special. Go! Create! Perform! And have fun.

On a final note ... I always give my flower away when my routine is done. Look to your audience. Who is laughing the most? Give your flower to that person ... and pass on the magic.

That is what being a Maker Magician is all about.

★ROUTINE: PAPER CAMERA

> **NOTE:** This routine was inspired by *Encyclopedia of Impromptu Magic* by Martin Gardner, "Camera," page 443

THE EFFECT

Just like the flower, this routine gives you a chance to be lighthearted and funny. Just as it sounds, it's a homemade paper "camera." You pretend to take a picture of someone with it, and a picture of them appears on the camera!

SUPPLIES

- **1 index card** Any size will work.
- **Scissors or X-Acto knife**
- **Crayons, markers, or colored pencils for tissue flower variation**

BUILD

1. Take an index card and fold it in half widthwise, like a hamburger (Figure **A**).

2. Place the folded card on a flat surface, with the open end facing you. Draw an outline of a square on one side of the folded card, making sure to leave at least ½" of margin at the bottom of the card. Take a dark marker and thicken the square outline (Figure **B**).

3. Now, we need to cut the two vertical lines of the square. With the help of a grown-up, you can do this with an X-Acto knife. Or, if using scissors, bend the crease of the folded card down toward the open end, but DO NOT crease it this time. Take your scissors and snip along the vertical lines of the square, cutting right through the double layer (Figures **C**, **D**, and **E**).

4. Open the card. One half of the card has your square drawing. The other half doesn't.

5. Now, we need to make two more cuts:
• On the outlined square, cut

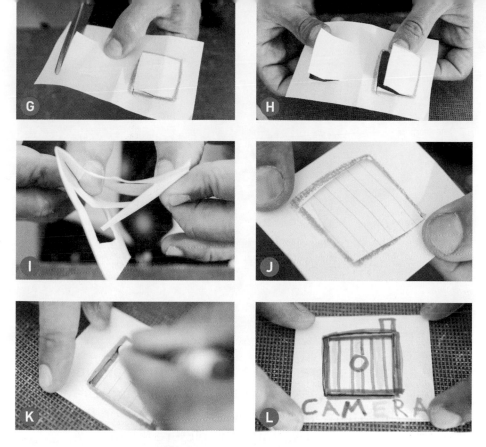

the line closest to the crease, creating a flap (Figure **F**).
- On the other half of the card, create another flap, cutting from line to line farthest from the crease (Figures **G** and **H**).

6. Now, re-fold the index card hamburger, but this time tuck the back flap in front of the front flap (Figures **I** and **J**).

7. We need to camouflage the flap on the front of our camera. Darken the outline of the square, making sure the outline covers the cuts (Figure **K**).

8. Now it's time to make it look like a camera! Draw a circle in the center for a lens and add a button on top (Figure **L**). Get creative and decorate it however you'd like!

9. Open your index card again, releasing the folds from their tucked position. You'll now see an empty space inside the

outline of your "camera." That's where we draw our "photo."
Let's say we plan on "taking a picture" of a person. Draw a
person in the empty space! Color a thick square on the inside
part of the card as well, framing the picture (Figure **M**).

10. When your drawing is done, refold the card, and re-tuck
the flaps. Now you're in performance position. The outside
of the card should appear as a camera, and the photo will be
hidden within.

THE PERFORMANCE
1. Say, "I need everyone to smile really big! I want to take a
picture of the person who is smiling like a movie star like me!"
(Make a big, crazy, silly smile.)

2. Take out your paper camera, and say, "This is my paper
camera (Figure **N**)! It can take a picture of you! Watch!"

3. Point the camera at someone who is smiling big, and say,
"Look at the camera! Say cheese! Everyone count to three!
One ... two ... three!"

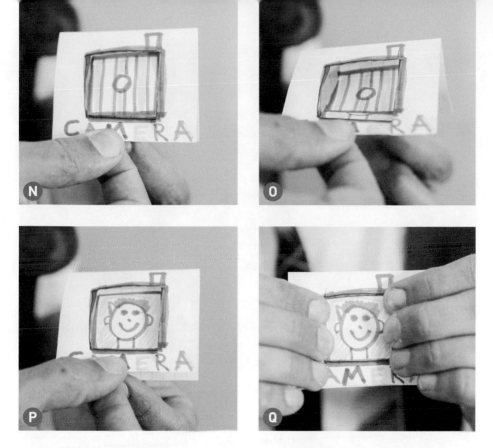

4. As everyone says three, you shout "cheese!" and at the same time, swiftly open and close the paper camera, releasing the tucked flaps. Boom! The paper face appears (Figures **O** and **P**)!

5. As you show the picture to the audience, hold the camera with your fingers along the side of the picture, helping to conceal the secret a bit and keeping the slits in the card less visible (Figure **Q**).

Have fun with this! Make a giant camera out of poster board! Think of different ways you can use this principle and different objects you can take pictures of. I've seen paper cameras that turn people into emojis! Use this camera concept to create new ideas!

★ROUTINE: PAPER STREAMER WAND

THE EFFECT

The magician appears onstage twirling a streamer on a stick in celebration. But — *oh no!* — the end of the streamer catches under his foot, and he accidentally rips it in half! In frustration, he rips the rest of the streamer off of the stick, tears it all to pieces, and crumples it up into a ball, only to wave the stick and reveal a restored streamer, attached to the stick once again. Victory!

This is a trick I perform in my own stage show! Here's how you do it.

SUPPLIES

- **1 roll of crepe paper streamers**
- **Masking or painters tape**
- **1 unsharpened pencil**

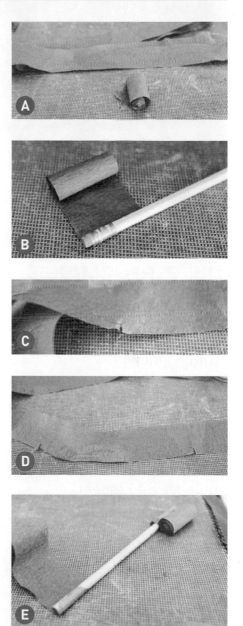

BUILD
PREP YOUR WAND

1. Tear off two 4' lengths of streamer from the roll. Roll up one of the 4' lengths of streamer, leaving a 2" tail (Figure **Ⓐ**).

2. Tape the end of the streamer to one end of the pencil (Figure **Ⓑ**).

3. In the other 4' length of streamer, make small tears every 12" to 18" or so on each side. This will help the streamer break during performance (Figures **Ⓒ** and **Ⓓ**).

4. In the same manner that you attached the rolled-up streamer to the pencil, fasten the un-rolled streamer to the other end of the pencil, taping the end and securing it (Figure **Ⓔ**).

THE PERFORMANCE

1. Pick up the streamer pencil wand with the rolled-up coil hidden in your hand (Figure **F**).

2. Twirl the streamer around with the wand (Figure **G**).

3. Twirl it close to your audience and repeat "Whatever you do, DO NOT, I REPEAT DO NOT grab this party streamer!" Say it over and over again, insinuating that you want someone to grab it. Someone will

"accidentally" pull and tear the streamer, ripping it in half (Figure **H**).

4. In frustration, say, "OH NO! My special rock star party streamer is BROKEN!" Rip off the rest of the streamer (Figures **I** and **J**).

5. Rip the two pieces up even more.

6. Then slowly crumple them into a ball in the hand that is not holding the wand while you continue to wave the wand around in the air with the other hand (Figure **K**).

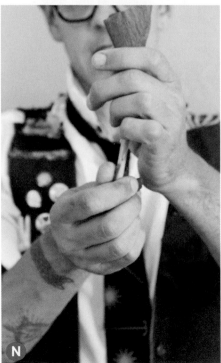

7. For the restoration, with a *swift* motion, touch the end of the pencil to the ball of crumpled-up streamer in your other hand (Figure **L**), and slide your hand (containing the second streamer) to the other end of the pencil (Figures **M** and **N**), allowing the rolled-up, intact streamer on the other end to reveal itself (Figure **O**).

You can roll pieces of hand cut confetti in with the rolled-up streamer, for a more dramatic restoration reveal.

8. This is a BIG moment! Swirl the restored streamer in excitement and celebrate with your favorite dance move and take your well deserved bow (Figure **P**)!

№5
THE FINALE

The music starts. It's upbeat and exciting, melodic and fun, and it makes you want to jump to your feet and move! You bring out a homemade bag filled with colorful fabric loops. You hand some out to different people, and when the bag is empty, you turn the bag inside out to show everyone that there's nothing there. You collect the loops back from everyone and have your audience wiggle their fingers at the bag. Then, you pull out one of the loops. But it's attached to another loop! And that one is attached to another one. Slowly, you keep pulling, and a whole chain of loops is revealed. At the end of the chain, a banner pops out. "THE END!" it says, and you take your well deserved applause with a bow.

★ROUTINE: LOOPS FINALE

THE EFFECT
In a split second, transform a pile of craft loops into one long craft loop chain!

SUPPLIES
- **3 different pairs of socks** The wilder the patterns and colors, the better!
- **1 discarded adult large T-shirt**
  alternative: material by the yard, if you have it
- **1 discarded adult large button down dress shirt**
- **Sewing machine (if you have one) and thread**
  alternative: sewing needle and dental floss or thread
- **Safety pins**
- **2 quarters/coins**
- **Acrylic paint + brushes**
- **Hot glue gun + glue**
- **Scissors**
- **Masking tape**

BUILD
CREATE THE BAG
We're going to make a bag out of a T-shirt! But this is no ordinary bag. This bag hides a secret ... it's actually two bags in one!

1. First, we'll need to cut three pieces of fabric from our T-shirt, each around 9"× 9" in size (Figure **A**).

2. Stack all three pieces of

A

fabric on top of each other, and sew them together on three sides (Figure **B**). Now you have a bag with two compartments. Trim any excess fabric and set your bag aside.

CUT THE LOOPS

1. Split your socks in two piles, with one sock from each pair in each pile.

2. We are going to cut your socks into loops! (Or donuts, or, if you're Italian like me ... calamari!)

3. Start with one pile of socks ... cut each sock entirely into approximately 1" horizontal strips (Figure **C**), which should result in loops of sock (Figure **D**). Stretch each loop out (Figures **E** and **F**), and they'll resemble craft loops (Figure **G**).

4. Do the same with the other pile of socks, but keep the piles separate. We'll want to have somewhere around 13–17 loops in each pile.

5. Set one pile aside. From the other pile, connect two loops, using a loop-to-loop knot method. Set the two connected loops aside (Figures **H** through **L**). Make a longer chain of loops with the remainder from that pile, again connecting the loops together using the loop-to-loop knot method (Figure **M**). Set aside for now.

MAKE THE BANNER
1. Moving on to the next element ... we need to create our "The End" banner. Cut an approximately 18"×13" rectangle from the discarded dress shirt.

2. Lay it flat, paint THE END on it, and decorate however you'd like (Figure **N**).

3. Let it dry, and add a safety pin on each top corner.

4. Flip the banner over and attach your coins to the bottom corners of the banner using hot glue (Figure **O**). This will help the banner unfold nicely when it's revealed from the bag during your performance!

5. Now, take your loop chain, and attach one end to a top corner of the banner, using a safety pin.

6. Take the two attached loops we had set aside earlier, and safety pin one end to the inside bottom corner of one compartment of our homemade bag. Safety pin the other end to the other top corner of the banner (Figure **P**).

7. Fold the banner like an accordion (Figure **Q**), from the bottom up, and carefully

slide it into the compartment of the bag that it is attached to (Figure **R** on the previous page).

8. Gather the loop chain, and slide it into the bag with the banner (Figure **S**). During the performance, you'll need to be able to easily find the loose end of the loop chain. Personally, I tie a double knot at the end, and have it resting on top of the loop chain pile, easy to distinguish and grab.

9. Now, take the pile of loose loops you set aside earlier, and place them in the other compartment in the bag (Figure **T**). Position your bag open with the side that contains the loose loops visible, and the other compartment closed, hiding the banner and loop chain.

THE PERFORMANCE

This routine works well with music! Select an upbeat track to work with!

1. Hold the bag with your hand clenching the hidden compartment closed, fingers in, thumb out. Allow the other compartment, with the loose loops, to be open. With your free hand, remove individual loose loops and hand them out to your audience (Figure ).

2. Walk back to your table with some loose loops still inside. Pull them out and show them separated and unattached. (Don't say it in words ... just with your actions.) Once the compartment is empty, stick your hand inside and turn the bag inside out.

3. Hit the bag onto your free hand with a clap, signifying that it is completely empty. Turn the bag back outside in, and lay it open on your table, still apparently empty to your audience.

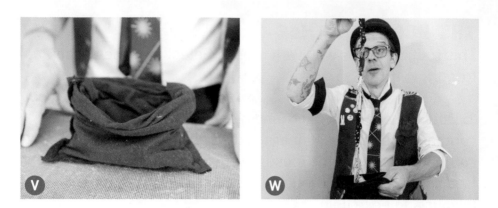

Make sure the full compartment is toward you and the empty compartment open and toward your audience (Figure **V**).

4. Collect all the loose loops from the audience and place them back in the empty compartment of the bag. When they're all in the bag, it's time to swiftly switch pockets, closing the bag and reopening the other side without the audience knowing the compartment is switched! They won't suspect that what they're seeing is anything other than the loops you just re-collected.

5. Wiggle your fingers over the bag. Have the audience wiggle their fingers! Take your time, enjoy the moment. The hard work is all done! You can say funny magic words, or ask if anyone has a magic wand. Take someone's shoe and wave it over the bag. Have fun!

6. When you're ready, take that double-knotted top loop and slowly tug it up (Figure **W**). Look surprised when you see that it's tied to another loop, slowly pull the chain up (Figure **X**). Adjust the bag as you do. Look more and more surprised. Say "WOW! This is CRAZY!" As it reaches the final loop, you'll see the banner start to show. Grab the bag now as you pull the chain. The banner will pull out and unfurl your "The End" message (Figure **Y**). Look at it with excitement! Look to the audience and take your well deserved bow!

№ 6
FINDING YOURSELF IN YOUR SHOW

What do you love? What are the things that make you happy? Take a moment. Make a list of 10 things. Ten things that make you smile when you think of them. Ten things that get you excited! Don't worry if they have nothing to do with magic ... that's not what matters here. When you are excited about something, the world will be excited with you. Think about how you can express your excitement for those things in your style and character. Maybe it's a song, a smell, or even a shirt you saw someone wear that made you say, "Wow! That shirt is awesome!" Think about the things that make you feel FREE. The more you think about those things, the more you will discover the unique story and style of YOU.

For me, the first time I saw video footage of Charlie Chaplin, the first time I went to a punk rock concert, the first time I skateboarded with friends ... those were all defining moments in my life. The first time I held an Arduino Uno, the first time I saw the movie *Benny and Joon*, the first time I saw *Hook*. What are those moments in your life?

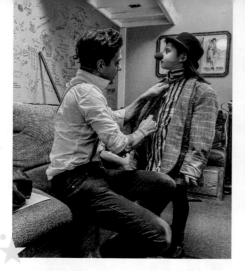

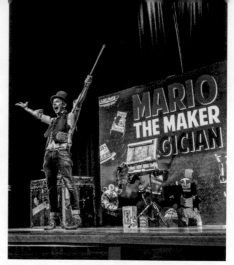

FINDING YOUR STYLE

The way we present ourselves outwardly as performers is important. It's the first impression our audience has of us. It helps define our character and our show. It's not just about what we wear, but also what our props look like, what our set-up looks like. The background, even the table, everything is important!

As you explore your style, don't think about what you think people expect to see in a magician. Think about what makes you — you alone — feel free. Have you ever had a day where the outfit you were wearing just made you feel so happy? That's your style! It's in there. A soon as I stopped caring about what I thought people wanted magicians to wear, I started to find my own freedom in style.

FINDING YOUR CHARACTER

Look at what makes you laugh! Look at the performers
who affect you the most. They have some of your character
in them! The desire to emulate someone else comes from
the fact that part of you is in there! What do you do with
that feeling? Use it to find yourself! As you start performing
you'll see patterns ... ways of interacting with your audience
that work and feel natural to you. Look at the things people
laughed at. The moments where people were amazed and
you felt it! Write them down. Write down the good and the
bad. Try to figure out why the good stuff is good, so you can
expand on it.

Keep in mind, though, never to judge a routine by a single
performance. There might be a good trick you do a few times,
but one time someone figures out the secret and shouts it
out. Don't give up on that trick! Fix what might have given
the secret away and try again. The best way to find your
character is to perform the same material over and over, so
it's memorized deep inside. From there, the fun begins.

Take the routines in this book and memorize the mechanics
through and through. They are hand picked because they
work! Do them over and over again. Build each prop from this
book with love. Perform each routine as much as you can ... so
much that you don't even have to think about the mechanics of
the trick anymore. Then you can fully focus on taking chances

at being silly and having fun and finding yourself on stage ... that is where your character lives!

As a performer, it's almost like you have to prove to your audience that you are worth watching. Once you've crossed that line, once you've done the hard work of learning the routines through and through, only then can you start to discover your character. And actually, the truth is, your audience creates your character. It comes from the small moments you discover that really, really work in your show. If you continually adapt and shape those moments, your character will slowly evolve with each performance.

Personally, looking back, I've realized that the things I feared most about performing are the things that actually ended up defining my character. It used to be that when I tried to perform serious magic, I would get really, really nervous. So nervous, that I would drop props and stumble on my words. I remember one show where I started sweating so much that whatever I held in my hands would slip right out! Looking back, I realized it was because I was not performing in a way that was true to me. In the mistakes, I found my character. It wasn't until someone laughed when I dropped something that I realized that could actually be funny intentionally. I started to understand a whole world of performing called slapstick comedy. Dropping things, and being clumsy, and nervous ... on purpose! Once I learned that being nervous and clumsy can be part of my character, I wasn't nervous anymore! I just pretended to be! What a relief! My fears became my strength.

BUILDING THEMES IN YOUR SHOW

How do we build a theme? I always look to the past first. Classic themes help shape modern ones. If you look at classic circus imagery, you'll see a lot of red, for example. A theme could be a strong color that's used throughout your performance. I love red! I have a red silk flower on my vest. I use red throughout my show in various ways. Think about your favorite colors. Build on those colors. Shapes can create themes too. I love stars. I put stars everywhere! I cut them out of cardboard,

I draw them on paper, I paint them. Having stars can be a theme. In my show I build the props to reflect the things I love. You could have a superhero theme! Every prop you build from the book could have superhero images on it. Every trick you do could have superhero jokes! You could wear a superhero mask and cape for your show! That's a theme!

I love minibikes, punk rock, and old hot rods ... loud engines and Rat Fink! So how do I create a theme with these things? Well, the back of my vest has punk rock patches. The front of my vest has buttons and pins with my interests on them. VWs, Maker Faire, and robots. My performance table is made from an old drum stand and vintage suitcase. My suitcase is covered with lots of stickers! Stickers from my travels, stickers from graffiti artists, and from fellow makers. That's a theme! What if you love skateboards? Imagine making a skateboard into a tabletop to perform on! Maybe it can clip to a drum stand like mine. Take what you love and let it reflect in everything you use in your show. There are no rules!

FINDING YOUR HUMOR

The more you perform, the more you'll notice what people laugh at. You'll shift into the direction of what gets the laugh. It's like a flower growing towards the sun ... no matter what, it will always bend and turn toward the sunlight. That's how it grows. Same with you. Listen to your audience! Listen to people reacting to other performances and other forms of entertainment and interaction. Pay attention to what makes people laugh. Carry a small notebook and pen, and write things down throughout the day. Maybe something happened that was accidentally funny. Write it down! Maybe you can somehow copy that accident in your show! There are natural funny things happening all the time. Those moments make the best comedy! The people who pay attention to that create amazing things. For me, I love when something gets stuck, or someone slips and falls down. I can naturally do it because it happens to me all the time. Watch The Three Stooges, The Great Ballantine, and Bill Irwin. They all have amazing ways of making people laugh.

USING MUSIC BEFORE, DURING, AND AFTER YOUR SHOW

It's been said that the moment someone enters a theater, the show has already started. Everything you see and do even just leading up to finding your seat can affect the experience. By adding a track of music as people get ready to see your performance, you're helping to create a vibe, an energy to the room. That vibe is the beginning of your theme! For me and my show everything is robots and electronic based, so I play retro video game music with robot sounds. It gives people a little clue into what will happen.

Music is such a powerful tool for performance! It can also fill important empty spaces in your show, like when you need a helper for a trick. Having music kick on as you search for a helper can fill what would be dead time, and transform it into something more enjoyable to watch. It can even be funny! Having the same silly song play each time you pick a helper can help create a recurring joke.

Music can help create mood, too, and elevate the routines you perform. It's one of the real secrets that many performers overlook. Don't overlook music! Every routine I do in my stage show has some sort of music at some point.

Music is especially helpful for transitions. Transitions are what you do as you go from one routine to the next. There are a lot of ways to do it. We can just throw the props from the previous trick into our case and pull the next trick out. Or maybe we can introduce the next trick without the audience even knowing! That would be called a smooth transition. This is all up to you, depending on your style and character. I've learned over the years that the more I stick to a specific style and character, the easier it is to find the right music.

BRINGING IT ALL TOGETHER

I want my audience to feel excited to be at my show. I love robots and making things with cardboard. I love skateboards and graffiti. I love artists like Basquiat and Andy Warhol. It makes sense, then, that when I perform, I wear torn up jeans and a vest with patches. My top hat is kind of beat up and worn in. My music is loud and melodic. Punk rock, rock 'n' roll. My props for my show have stickers on them from street artists I love. A lot of my props have cardboard and bright colors! Robots everywhere! Through this book, I hope you find that the tricks are just the beginning ... they are opportunities. Opportunities to find your character, style, music ... to find who YOU are as a performer.

★ PROJECT: CREATE A BACKDROP

As you begin performing you will also begin to realize that every small detail in and around your show has the power to help or hurt you. A backdrop might be something you never thought of as important, but it is! This is another detail that can help elevate your show. Why? Remember ... the show really does start the moment the audience walks into the theater. This theater might be your living room or a classroom. We want to help guide your audience's perception. Having a handmade backdrop will create intrigue right from the start, and that energy will help you believe in yourself, too!

The backdrop can be simple and still say a lot, and the design possibilities are vast. Curtains! Stars! Robots! Emojis! You'll have to experiment, and that's part of the fun. For my example here, I'm making a giant robot head!

SUPPLIES
- **1 flat bedsheet** any size, in your choice of color
- **Acrylic paint + brushes**
- **Sewing machine + thread**
- **Lots of cardboard**
- **Thumb tacks for hanging the backdrop**
- **Hot glue gun + hot glue**
- **Tape measure**
- **Scissors**
- **Optional: dental floss + curved sewing needle**

BUILD
CREATE DECORATIONS

1. Lay your sheet down flat. Cut some stars out of cardboard, and place them loosely around on the sheet to see where they look best. I made a robot head using multiple pieces of cardboard together.

2. Paint your stars!

3. Paint your robot!

ATTACH DECORATIONS

There are two ways I like to connect the cardboard to the sheet. Hot glue will work. Or you can sew them on with dental floss and a curved sewing needle! Dental floss is strong, easy to sew with, and comes in a container with a built-in cutter! It's a true maker tool! Using a curved needle, you can sew the stars and robot to the sheet.

№ 7
ROBOTS & MAGIC

There are three "maker superpowers" that I love to use as a Maker Magician. They are: 3D designing, 3D printing my designs, and then animating them with microcontrollers. This can all sound overwhelming and confusing at first, but I promise you, you can learn them, and once you do, the possibilities really do become endless.

Being able to *create* what you *imagine* is powerful. The idea of creating something that can move by itself is freeing. The idea of making a robot sidekick, or a robot that performs a card trick with you, is amazing! Imagine a robot that can tell a joke with you and get an audience to laugh. That's so cool! How do we do these things? Well, it all starts with learning how to design what you imagine.

SUPERPOWER №1

3D design is our first maker superpower. Tinkercad.com is a great example of one simple yet powerful 3D design tool that is completely free. You can go online and sign up right now! Tinkercad includes built-in tutorials right on their site, so you can start using their program right away. It's free. It's accessible. It's easy to learn. I've seen kindergarteners using Tinkercad and creating amazing things! The more you use a program like this, the more comfortable you'll be. Tinkercad is just one example, but there are many 3D design program options out there. Start small, start simple with your designs, and build up from there.

SUPERPOWER №2

The second maker superpower is 3D printing! This is how you take the thing you designed on your computer screen, in Tinkercad or another 3D design program, and make it into a tangible, physical three-dimensional object that you can actually hold in your hands! A 3D printer is like a hot glue gun that moves around, melting and pushing out a thread of spaghetti-like plastic. That's right! A roll of plastic spaghetti

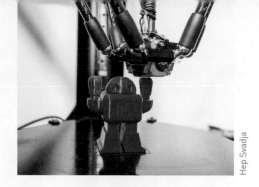
Hep Svadja

on a spool goes through a heated nozzle and creates your object layer by layer. It's amazing to watch! It's definitely a maker superpower to be able to 3D print what you imagine. If you are not able to have a 3D printer in your home, check your local libraries, schools, and makerspaces. Every major city and most smaller cities and towns have them available for use somewhere!

Another thing to keep in mind is that there are lots of people out there who share their 3D designs for others to use. Go to thingiverse.com and look around! You can print their designs just as they created them, or you can take them, modify them yourself, and then print them! You don't always have to start completely from scratch. One of the best things about the maker community is their willingness to share!

SUPERPOWER №3

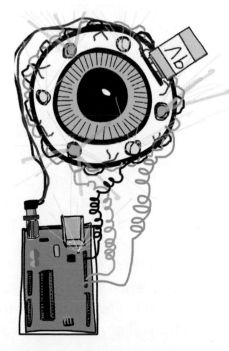

Our third maker superpower is programming microcontrollers. That's how all of my robots move and perform magic in my stage show. In the beginning of my show, I have banners and signs all appear on my case. I have flags that pop up and spring snakes that shoot out. It's electronic chaos, and it's my favorite part of the show. The robotics take over, and I use programming and microcontrollers to make people laugh!

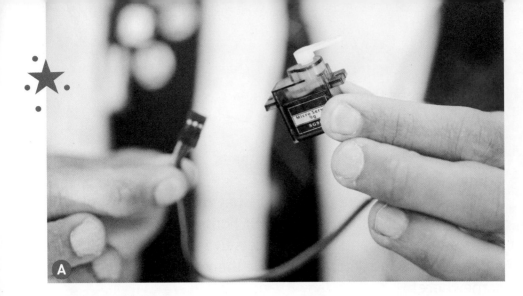

A

The Arduino Uno microcontroller is a blue credit card-sized board that costs under $30. It has 13 digital pins. That means you can plug in and control 13 different things. I love servomotors (Figure Ⓐ). They are magic! Buy an Arduino kit and a few micro servos along with some 22-gauge solid core wire, wire cutters, and wire strippers, and you can get started. Almost all of the physical animations in my show move because of servomotors. A servo is a little plastic box with a flat plastic arm attached that can move 180°. Imagine making miniature flags pop up behind your shoebox, or fuzzy rabbit ears that pop out of a hat and then hide again. That can all be created with an Arduino and a servomotor. The Arduino runs on 9 volts. That means it's portable! You can build something electronic that fits in your shoebox ... or in an old suitcase like me.

Arduino runs on its own language and software. Once you purchase a board you can download the software for free online. It's open source and community based. Once downloaded, you can run example code and start tinkering. You can learn how to use the Arduino to make a servo move. You can learn how to use timing to make things happen in set sequence and at set intervals. That will open up so many possibilities for you! With Arduino, you can control when you want that servo arm to move, when you want it to stop, and how long to wait before it moves again. Having this control can create great comedy, great magic, and great storytelling.

You can attach all kinds of lightweight objects to a servo arm to create magic. In my show, the top of my hat opens up and a clown nose appears. I grab the nose, that hat closes, and then it repeats the action and the nose comes back. This is all done with servomotors and an Arduino. No strings or pulleys, just two little servomotors, some wire, and an Arduino Uno. I also have 3D printed elements that help accomplish the hat opening up and pushing the nose out.

The reason I call these things superpowers is because my constant dream as a performer, thinker, and person is to create what I imagine. No matter how hard it may seem, having these three skills will get you to your goal. Plus, it's a journey with great reward. You work through a lot of trial and error with these superpowers. Sometimes, I have to print the same piece six, seven, eight times, making small adjustments each time, before everything fits and works like I envisioned it. And when it finally works, it's the greatest feeling in the world! You took the challenge on your own. You stuck to it, you didn't give up. You pushed yourself to learn something new. You are never too young, or too old, to learn new things. These three maker superpowers have shaped and changed my career and confidence.

This is just the beginning. You can add remote control with an Arduino too! You can plug in sensors! Imagine a table. Imagine if anytime you put something on that table, the table tilts itself over and drops the object on the floor!

I built a table like that using servomotors and a 3D printed pan and tilt mechanism. It was super fun! When I first thought of that idea, I didn't yet have the means to build it. I didn't yet have the skills to realize the idea. I wrote it down and let it go. But once I learned the three magic maker superpowers … wow, what freedom! I was able to revisit that old table idea and make it a reality. Now, I am only limited by my imagination. That's what I want for you, too!

Another concept I want to introduce you to is the idea that you don't have to create something completely from scratch. You can take things that already exist and HACK them to make them your own! Let's talk about ...

HACKING BATTERY POWERED TOYS!

To hack something means to take it apart and put it back together in a brand new way. You already know about servomotors. You should also know about relays. A relay can turn anything electronic *on* or *off* with just a little bit of electricity! A 5V relay can be attached to an Arduino. You can carefully take apart and open up a battery powered toy. Every battery powered toy has a switch. That switch will have two wires coming out of it. When the toy is *on*, the wires connect through the switch. When the toy is *off*, the wires separate inside the switch. You can actually clip the two wires from the switch and attach it to a relay, which is in turn attached to your Arduino. Now, you can control the on and off switch through the Arduino, without touching the toy!

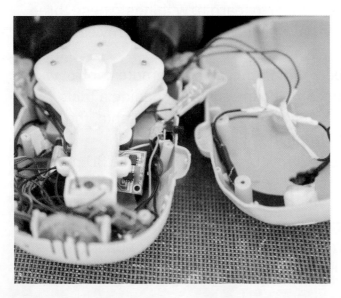 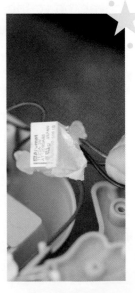

You might be saying, "Big deal, Mario, who cares?"

Well, what if you timed a magic trick to the code you programmed on the Arduino?

HERE'S AN EXAMPLE:

I have someone pick a playing card. They memorize it. I introduce a cheapo dancing robot toy that I picked up at an inexpensive local store.

"This toy robot will read your mind! Concentrate on your chosen card!" I say as I wave a playing card over the robot toy. It lights up for just a quick moment.

"Oh my! Is this your card?" I ask. It's not their card. I take a second card and try again. The robot mysteriously lights up again for just a slight moment. "Is this your card?" I ask. Again, it's not their card.

Now, I'm scrambling and a bit confused ... I grab one more card in desperation, hover it over the toy robot's head and BOOM! It springs to life, lighting up with sound and movement!

"Is THIS your card?!" I exclaim! "YES!" they say. And with that, I dance right along with the toy robot in celebration!

This is just one simple example of how attaching a relay to a manufactured electronic toy can create an amazing magic trick. Any battery powered toy can be connected to a relay and an Arduino. Learning some simple Arduino code can go a long way! Servomotors and relays are huge secret weapons in the Maker Magician toolbox. Add that to 3D design and 3D printing, and well, we can take over the world with our maker magic!

WRAP UP

After reading this book, I want you to realize that you *can* create what you imagine. Let your ideas guide you toward trying new things and learning new skills. That is what it means to be a Maker Magician.

And remember ... cardboard and crayons are just as important as 3D printers and Arduino. Keep creating. Keep making magic. Adapt what we've created together in this book, and make it your own. Take it to new levels. Invent new tricks altogether!

And in every aspect of life ...

DO WHAT YOU LOVE.

USE WHAT YOU HAVE.

AND ALWAYS ... HAVE FUN.

⭐ ABOUT THE AUTHOR: ⭐

Mario "the Maker Magician" Marchese is a touring performer with an all-ages theater show full of homespun magic, DIY robotics, and punk rock slapstick. It's magic through the lens of the Maker Movement! He has appeared on *Sesame Street*, NBC's Universal Kids, and live on tour with David Blaine, who calls him "the best kids' magician in the world!!"

Mario travels the country and world with his show, along with his co-adventurer Katie, and their children, Gigi and Bear. They are dedicated to road-schooling and learning through exploration. It's a family business through and through. When not touring, they create an innovative online version of their show from their home base in Nyack, New York.

In their cover story about Mario, *M-U-M Magazine* called him "magic's punk rock Peter Pan philosopher."

We'd be hard-pressed to put it better than that.